26 Fairmount Avenue

written and illustrated by

Tomie dePaola

SCHOLASTIC INC.
New York Toronto London Auckland Sydney
Mexico City New Delhi Hong Kong

ISBN 0-439-17315-9

12 11 10 9 8 7 6 5 4 3 2 1   0 1 2 3 4 5/0

Printed in the U.S.A.   23

First Scholastic printing, September 2000

Book design by Donna Mark. Text set in Garth Graphic.

*For my wonderful, wacky family and relatives,
especially Flossie; friends and old neighbors in
Meriden, Connecticut; and my longtime assistant,
Bob Hechtel, who has helped and put up
with me for years and whose idea it was
for me to do this book.*

Mom

Dad

Nana

Tom

Uncle Charles+Viva

the Morins

Buddy

Me

Aunt Nell

Nana Fall-River

Mr. + Mrs. Crane

Carol Crane

COLUMBUS AVE.

Chapter One

I didn't always live in the house at 26 Fairmount Avenue. We moved there when I was
five years old. I know that because in 1938,
when I was still four, a big hurricane hit
Meriden, Connecticut, where we lived. We
had just started to build our first and only
house, when people told my mom and
dad that the house was twisting and
turning on its foundation, just like
Dorothy's house in *The Wizard*
of Oz. A real hurricane had
never reached all the way up
to New England before, so
nobody was ready for it.

We were living in an apartment on Columbus Avenue. We all lived on one floor. Another family lived upstairs, and we lived downstairs.

It had been raining for days and days, and some of the rivers were overflowing. There was a really weird brook near our backyard. It was called Harbor Brook. It wound all the way through Meriden, and factories dumped stuff in it. It was different colors on different days. We were told NOT TO GO NEAR IT. Right before the hurricane, the water was so high and murky that I was hardly allowed to *look* at it, much less go near it. "Come away from there, Tomie," my mom would call.

Right after lunch on the day of the hurricane, my mom was talking on the telephone when my dad came home early from the barbershop, where he worked. My brother, Buddy, who was eight, was at school. (His real name was Joe Jr., after my father.) Dad and Mom talked in the kitchen. Then Mom said to me, "Get your coat on, Tomie. We have to go

pick up Buddy and some of the neighborhood
children. There's a big storm coming, and
they're letting everyone out early."

We got in the car and drove to the
school in the rain. A long line
of cars and teachers with
kids were waiting in
front of the building.
I looked up and saw
something I've never
ever forgotten.

A boy was standing
at the top of the steps,
holding an umbrella.
All of a sudden a gust of
wind blew, a really strong
gust, and the boy went up,
up, up in the air and floated
down the stairs just like
Mary Poppins.

It was scary driving
home to Columbus Avenue,
the car filled with kids—

Buddy, Carol Crane (my best friend on Columbus Avenue, who looked just like the child movie star Shirley Temple, only Carol had red hair and Shirley Temple was blonde), the Adams twins, the Fournier brothers, and a few others—all talking and screaming. Branches fell off the trees, leaves swirled around the car. A sign flew off Tomasetti's grocery store and just missed us. But we made it to our apartment. Mom let us out, and we ran inside. Carol's mother, Mrs. Crane, was already there, and she was really scared.

Mrs. Crane was scared of storms, especially thunderstorms. If there was one clap of thunder, Mrs. Crane would be knocking on our door and calling my mother. "Floss, Floss!" (That was my mother's nickname, for Florence. My mother liked being called Floss, but she liked Flossie even better!) My mom would open the door, and Mrs. Crane would rush in, pushing Carol in front of her. Nothing would

4

do except for my mom to get the bottle of Holy Water she'd gotten from Saint Joseph's Church and sprinkle some of it on Mrs. Crane, who wasn't even Catholic. I guess she thought that Catholic Holy Water was better than nothing, and it must have worked because Mrs. Crane never got struck by lightning.

On the day of the hurricane, my mom calmed Mrs. Crane down and promised she'd get the Holy Water, while my dad parked the car where there were no trees. First Mom lit some candles because the electricity was out. Then she took the Holy Water and sprinkled some on Mrs. Crane. Everyone else wanted to be sprinkled, too.

Mr. and Mrs. Morin and their daughter, Althea, who lived in the apartment upstairs, came down. I guess they thought, with all the voices and everything, that it was a party.

We crowded around the windows and listened to the wind howl and watched it blow stuff all over the yard—tree limbs, lawn furniture, garbage cans, even a birdbath. Then it got really quiet. We looked up and saw a little, round patch of blue sky through the dark clouds. "That's the eye of the hurricane," my dad told us. I didn't see any eye, but before I could say anything, the wind picked up and the rain started all over again.

"I hope the new house is okay," my dad said as the wind roared by like a freight train.

My mom pulled a book off the shelf and started reading a story to Buddy, Carol, the Adams twins, the Fournier brothers, and yours truly, just as she read to Buddy and me every night.

Finally, three hours later, the Hurricane of 1938 was over. People started coming out of their houses. "Do you have electricity?" someone shouted. "No, do you?" someone answered.

I pestered my mom so much that she let me go outside with Carol, her father, Buddy, and my dad. Branches, large and small, and leaves were everywhere. We could hear sirens wailing. We walked to Hemlock Grove, a small forest of tall hemlock trees at the end of the block.

It was a mess. "Be careful. I don't think it's all that safe," one of the neighbors told us. Trees had fallen in all directions, criss-crossing each other like a giant game of pick-up-sticks. Some of those trees stayed there for a long time, and after we moved into 26 Fairmount Avenue and I felt brave, I'd take the shortcut to Columbus Avenue through Hemlock Grove. One tree lay across a little stream, and if you had good balance you could walk across it.

I guess 1938 was a special year. Not only because of the hurricane, but because it was the year we started building 26 Fairmount Avenue.

Chapter Two

When my mom and dad decided to build a house, friends told them that they were building "out in the sticks." That meant way out where not many people lived. There wasn't even a real street. Just a dirt road. But it wasn't that far from our apartment on Columbus Avenue.

It was really great watching the house being built. First a steam shovel dug a huge hole for the foundation. Next a cement truck came, and workers poured the cement down a chute that looked like a long sliding board.

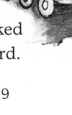

I pretended that the concrete gushing down was lava coming out of a volcano (I had seen that in a movie with my mother).

After the foundation was set and the cellar was finished, the builders came to start on the house itself. They covered the opening over the cellar with wood, and that became the floor. Then they put up these things they called "studs," which were pieces of wood called "two-by-fours" because they are two inches thick by four inches wide.

They had just finished this part of the house when the hurricane struck. It was a good thing the walls weren't up yet, because the house probably would have blown away. A new house a few streets away was knocked down by the wind. All that was left was the cellar and a mess of broken wood. They had to start all over again. It was sad, but I was glad it wasn't our house.

All our relatives were excited about the house at 26 Fairmount Avenue. I guess a new house with a big yard and a view of West Peak with Castle Craig on top was exciting. I know I thought it was.

We had both Irish and Italian relatives in our family because my mom was Irish and my dad was Italian. The Irish relatives came to visit the most because they lived in Wallingford, which wasn't too far from Meriden. Some of the Italian relatives lived up in Massachusetts, and some down in the Bronx, in New York City.

I was pretty lucky because I had one grandfather, two grandmothers, and a great-grandmother. But my grandmothers and my great-grandmother were all called Nana, and that was confusing to me. And then there was this "great" business.

But I figured out what to call them, and everyone always knew who I was talking about.

I called my Irish great-grandmother Nana Upstairs, because she spent all of her time upstairs. She was ninety-four years old. I called my Irish grandmother Nana Downstairs, because if she wasn't helping Nana Upstairs, she was either in the kitchen or sitting in her chair in the parlor, looking out the window so she'd know what was going on in the neighborhood. My Italian grandmother lived in Fall River, Massachusetts, so I called her Nana Fall River.

I called my Irish grandfather Tom, because he told me to. "Tomie will be grown up before he can say 'Grandpa,'" he told my mom. "He can call me Tom." So I did.

Every Sunday we went down to Wallingford. As soon as we arrived, I always ran upstairs. Upstairs was a special place for me, and my Nana Upstairs was a special person to me. I loved her, and every Sunday I spent all my time with her.

Nana Downstairs would help Nana Upstairs into the big Morris chair next to her bed. She'd take out a long cloth and gently tie Nana Upstairs in her chair so she wouldn't fall out.

I pestered and pestered Nana Downstairs until she tied me in a chair, too. But she'd put the knot in front so that if I got tired of being in the chair I could get down and poke around or go to the bathroom or something. When I heard her coming up the stairs, I'd climb back into the chair. I got pretty good at tying the knot back, and she never came into the room until I was ready. It was Nana Downstairs' and my private game.

I loved to look around Nana Upstairs' room. She had beautiful brushes and combs and glass jars that held her big silvery hairpins on top of her dresser. Sometimes I'd find candy mints or Life Savers in the sewing box on the table out in the hall.

One Sunday I opened the sewing box and there was no candy, only needles and thread and buttons. So I went searching, very quietly. Finally I got to the bathroom. I stood on the wooden toilet seat and opened up the

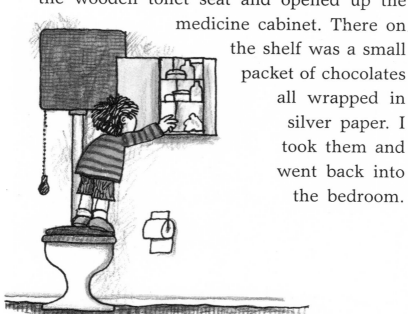

medicine cabinet. There on the shelf was a small packet of chocolates all wrapped in silver paper. I took them and went back into the bedroom.

I tied myself back in my chair, and Nana Upstairs and I ate the chocolates—all of them.

Well, those chocolates weren't chocolates at all. They were laxatives, and laxatives make you go to the bathroom a lot. Both Nana Upstairs and I didn't feel so good, and I think we both made a mess.

Nana Downstairs never forgot the mints or the Life Savers again.

Chapter Three

As exciting as beginning the new house and the big hurricane were, something I had been waiting for for a long time had happened in the spring of 1938. Mr. Walt Disney's movie *Snow White and the Seven Dwarfs* had come to Meriden.

My mother had read the true story of Snow White to my brother and me. I couldn't wait to see it in the movies. I thought Mr. Walt Disney was the best artist I had ever seen (I already knew that I wanted to be an artist, too). I loved his cartoons—especially "Silly Symphonies," Mickey Mouse, Donald Duck, and the Three Little Pigs. But now Mr. Walt Disney had done the first ever full-length animated movie—one and a half hours long.

I had been to a lot of movies—more than Buddy, even though he was eight. Because I didn't go to school yet, my mother took me with her to the movies in the afternoons. We both loved movies. My favorite real-life movie stars were Shirley Temple, the little girl with blonde curls who could sing and dance better than anyone, and Miss Mae West. (I called her "Miss" because she was grown up while Shirley Temple was about my age. We always called grown-ups Miss, Mr., or Mrs.) Miss Mae West was blonde, too, and she could sing. She didn't dance, but she was all shiny and glittery and all she had to do was walk and talk and everyone in the movie theater laughed and laughed.

17

Mom, Buddy, and I went to see *Snow White* on a Saturday. We got in line early at the Capitol Theatre so that we could get good seats. My mom bought the tickets, and as we went into the lobby, music was playing. She bought each of us a box of Mason's Black Crows—little chewy licorice candies (they didn't have popcorn at the movies yet).

We found our seats. The lights went down. First we saw a newsreel (it was all the real things that were going on in the world). After that was the coming attraction about the next movie that would be shown at the Capitol. And finally, with the sound of trumpets, and glittery stars filling the screen, the words I had been waiting for: "Feature Presentation."

A big book appeared on the screen with "Snow White and the Seven Dwarfs" on the front cover. The book opened. My mother read the words to me quietly: "Once upon a time..."

Music played, and there, in beautiful color, was Snow White, with white doves flying all around her. She was down on her knees, scrubbing the stairs in the Evil Queen's castle. Snow White asked the doves if they wanted to know a secret. They cooed yes. She told them they were standing by a wishing well. Then she sang a song about wishing for her prince to come.

WOW! I was really seeing *Snow White*, and it was the best movie I had ever seen.

Then the Prince came on the screen and sang to Snow White. The Evil Queen, looking fierce and mean, watched. My brother sank down in his seat.

The Evil Queen went to her Magic Mirror and said the words I knew so well: "Mirror, Mirror on the wall, who is the fairest of them all?" The mirror said it was Snow White, and the Evil Queen looked angrier than ever. Buddy sank down even farther.

19

But he really freaked out when the Evil Queen ordered the huntsman to take Snow White into the woods to be killed, and the woods looked just like Hemlock Grove. Tree limbs grabbed at Snow White, and yellow eyes stared down at her.

It was scary, and I loved it. But lots of kids didn't, and suddenly I heard crying and screaming all around me, even from Buddy.

"I want to go home!" he yelled.

"Come on," my mother said, standing up. "Let's go."

"I'm not going," I said. I had waited a long time for Mr. Walt Disney's movie. My mom, who is probably the smartest person in the world, understood. "All right, Tomie, sit right here and don't move. I'll be in the lobby with your brother." That was fine with me.

Lots of mothers left with their kids. I thought that was a good thing to do if the kids were afraid of the trees. They probably would wet their pants when the Evil Queen made the poisoned apple for Snow White and drank the magic potion to turn herself into the Evil Witch (even I was a little scared when that happened).

Then things about the story started to bother me. Why was the Evil Queen making the poisoned apple now? The true story was different. In that story, before the Evil Queen gave Snow White the apple, she went to the dwarfs' cottage and pulled the laces of Snow White's vest so tight that Snow White couldn't breathe and she fainted. The dwarfs came home just in time to loosen the laces and save her.

Next, the Queen went a second time to visit Snow White with a poison comb, which she stuck in Snow White's hair. Snow White fainted once more, but the dwarfs got back in time to take the comb out and save her again.

The *third* time was the poisoned apple.

Maybe Mr. Walt Disney hadn't read the true story, because he used only the apple. I stood up and shouted at the movie screen, "Where are the laces? Where is the comb?"

A lady behind me said, "Hush, little boy! Sit down." I did, and the movie was like the book again until the dwarfs put Snow White into the crystal coffin.

But then I knew that Mr. Walt Disney hadn't read the true story carefully enough because he got it all mixed up with "Sleeping Beauty" and had the Prince kiss Snow White, and she woke up. In the true story the Prince carries the coffin to his palace, and on the way the piece of poisoned apple falls out of Snow White's mouth and she wakes up. But this time I didn't yell at the movie screen, in case the lady behind me got mad at me again.

22

But when "The End" appeared on the screen, boy, was I mad! I couldn't help it. I stood up and hollered, "The story's not over yet. Where's the wedding? Where're the red-hot iron shoes that they put on the Evil Queen so she dances herself to death?"

That was the true end of the true story. Just then my mom came running in, grabbed me, and dragged me out.

"Mr. Walt Disney didn't read the story right," I yelled again.

I never did understand it, and when I went to see *Snow White and the Seven Dwarfs* again, with Carol Crane, I warned Carol that Mr. Walt Disney hadn't read the true story. I didn't yell at the movie screen. But I still wished I could have seen the Evil Queen dancing to death in those red-hot iron shoes!

Chapter Four

Right after the Christmas of 1938, my dad had a big fight with the man he had hired to build the house. My mom and dad wanted the house to be built a certain way, but the builder didn't listen to them. "I'm paying for it," Dad said. And they fired the builder.

So 26 Fairmount Avenue just sat there all winter without any work being done. My dad and mom would put Buddy and me in the car and drive by to look at the sad, unfinished house. Maybe we would have to live in apartments forever.

Easter came. Easter was always fun because every year the Easter Bunny brought Buddy and me Easter baskets. I always got a stuffed animal, too. My favorite was a duck.

We got new "outfits" to wear to church on Easter Sunday. My mom must have loved to dress up Buddy and me, because there are pictures and home movies of us, Buddy in long pants, a jacket, and necktie; me in shorts, a striped shirt, and a beret. We certainly were what grown-ups call "fashion plates."

"Guess what?" my dad said one day in the spring. "Johnny Papallo, Tony Nesci, and a few of my other friends are going to help us finish the house."

Hurray! I might get to live in our house at 26 Fairmount Avenue after all.

But before my dad's friends could start work, the City decided that Fairmount Avenue would be a real street with telephone poles and streetlights.

Machines came and scraped away lots of dirt, which made the street lower. Suddenly our house, which had been on a small hill, was way up in the air. My mom cried. My dad said some bad words.

Now a wall would have to be built to keep the front yard from falling into the street. Stairs would have to be made so we could get to the front door. And, last but not least, they would have to put in a steep driveway so we could get to the garage. Until all this was done, no one could work on the house because no one could get up to it.

And the new street was still just dirt. Every time it rained, the street turned to mud.

Well, my father's friends were really smart men. They just got boards and loads of wooden planks and made a long walkway up to the house. Mr. Johnny Papallo, Mr. Tony Nesci, and all the others started to work.

Soon the roof was on the house and the inside walls were up. They were made of plasterboard, which was like heavy cardboard. Later, men called "plasterers" would come and smear wet plaster over the plasterboard, and it would dry into smooth, white walls.

But before the plasterers came, Mr. Johnny Papallo gave me a piece of bright blue chalk from his toolbox. He knew I wanted to be an artist when I grew up. I looked at those blank walls and knew what I wanted to do.

I asked my mom if I could make drawings of the family on the walls. She and my dad talked about it, and finally my dad said, "Okay, Tomie. Mom and I decided that you can make pictures on the plasterboard. But as soon as the plasterers come, no more drawing on the walls. Okay?"

Sure, it was okay. But maybe if they saw how great my pictures were, they'd keep

them. I decided I would give each person in the family a special corner in what was going to be our living room.

I put Mom and Dad in a corner by the fireplace. I put my grandfather, Tom, in the other corner. (I put me there, too.) I put Buddy and Nana Downstairs and Nana Fall River by the kitchen. That way they wouldn't have far to go. (I didn't draw Nana Upstairs because she had died and gone to heaven a few months before.) The corner by the front door was for Uncle Charles and his girlfriend, Viva. Along the wall I drew some cousins, looking out the two windows.

We didn't have real stairs to the second floor yet, so I couldn't go up to the bedrooms. Mom had already told me that the biggest one was for her and Dad, and the smallest one was the just-in-case nursery. (Later we needed it for my sisters, Maureen and Judie.)

If I could have gotten up there I would have gone into the room Buddy and I were going to share and marked which side was mine. But that would have to wait.

The plasterers finally came and covered over all my beautiful drawings. I was mad

about that, but my grandfather, Tom, told me that was perfect because they'd always be there under the plaster and wallpaper. That made me feel better. Tom always made me feel better.

With everything moving along smoothly, my dad started talking about the "backyard project." The backyard was filled with weeds and tall grass and stuff. It would be plowed and smoothed so grass could be planted.

"I'm going to wait for fall to get here for the backyard project," Dad said. "Maybe we can start on the front wall and the steps up to the walkway to the front door."

But before they did, guess what? The City came back and scraped more and more dirt away from the street. Our house was even higher up in the air than before, and we needed the wall more than ever.

My mom kept crying. My dad kept using more and more bad words.

Chapter Five

In the fall of 1939, almost one year after the Hurricane of 1938, I started school. I was hoping that I could say my address was 26 Fairmount Avenue, but not yet.

I was excited about going to school because I knew that in school you learned to read. I really wanted to learn so that I wouldn't always have to wait for my mom to read stories to me.

The first day of school came. I was going to be in the afternoon kindergarten class. My mom and I walked to King Street. At the corner, I said, "I know the way," (it was just down the street). "I want to go alone." My mom said I could. She watched me walk down the street. She waved when I reached the school.

I walked up the long front stairs where the boy with the umbrella had floated down during the hurricane. I didn't know that students weren't supposed to use those stairs. They were reserved for the president or the king of England and especially for the superintendent of schools.

I pulled open the heavy front door and went in. A lady was standing there. "Who are you, little boy?" she asked.

"I'm Tomie dePaola," I answered. "Who are you?"

"I'm Miss Burke, the principal." (I got to know her really well over the next seven years.)

Miss Burke told me not to use the front door again, and she showed me where the kindergarten room was.

The room was filled with kids crying and hanging onto their mothers. *Boy,* I thought, *what babies.* I didn't realize that I would be in school with those kids for years and years.

I went up to a lady who looked like she might be the teacher. She was.

"And who are we?" she asked. (She always used "we." "We must take our naps now," or "We must bring our chairs into a circle"—stuff like that.)

"I'm Tomie dePaola," I said.

"Oh, aren't we lucky," she said. "I had your big brother, Joseph, in kindergarten, too," (she was talking about Buddy). Well, I figured it wouldn't take too long for her to realize that my brother and I were *very* different. But that could wait.

"When do we learn how to read?" I asked.

"Oh, we don't learn how to read in kindergarten. We learn to read next year, in first grade."

"Fine," I said. "I'll be back next year." And I walked right out of the school and all the way home.

No one was there. My dad was working at the barbershop, and my mom was off shopping all by herself for the first time in a long while.

The school called my dad at the barbershop. He found my mom, and they came roaring home to Columbus Avenue.

There I was, holding one of my mom's big books, staring at it, hoping that I could learn to read by myself.

When I told Mom and Dad what had happened, my dad said, "You handle this one,
Floss." And he went back to work.

My mom sat down next to me. "You know,"
she said, "if you don't go to kindergarten, you
won't pass. And if you don't pass, you'll never
get into first grade, and you'll never learn to
read."

So I went back to school, but I never really
liked kindergarten.

Chapter Six

Now it was time to start "the backyard project." The first thing we had to do was to burn off all the stuff that was growing there. It was a Saturday, so Buddy and I weren't at school, and our friends and neighbors came to help. Carol Crane came, too.

It was a sunny day, with no wind blowing. "That's very important," my dad told us.

"Why?" I asked.

"Well, if it's windy, the fire could spread and the house might burn down." I sure didn't want that to happen.

"Okay," my dad said. "Let's begin!"

"All right kids," my mom said. "Stand back out of the way."

My dad, Mr. Tony Nesci, Mr. Johnny Papallo, Mr. Crane, and a bunch of other people stood around all three sides of the field with old brooms, buckets of water, and wet burlap bags. My mom stood holding a hose attached to the one water faucet that worked. Everyone was ready.

They lit the fire at the edges, and it blazed right up. They wet their brooms and put out the flames around the outside of the circle. They did such a good job keeping the flames low that the whole fire went out.

"Try again, Joe!" someone called to my dad. This time he lit the fire in the middle, and it caught and burned bright and strong. Everyone shouted, "Hurray!"

But then the smoke started to get in people's eyes. They ran from the edges. Suddenly the fire was really big. Everyone was shouting and banging the flames with wet brooms and burlap bags.

Brooms caught fire. Burlap bags caught fire. The smoke got thicker.

"Quick, Floss," my dad shouted. "The hose, the hose!"

"Buddy! Turn on the faucet!" Mom shouted. Water streamed out of the hose.

"Wet down the house," Uncle Charles yelled. My mom did.

"Put out the flames!" Mrs. Florence Nesci shouted. My mom aimed the hose at the fire.

She kept squirting water all over the place until the fire was out. What a mess!

The weeds and grasses were black and smoking. So were the people. Everyone had black, sooty faces and smoky clothes. And everyone except my mom was soaking wet.

"Look what you've done to us," Mr. Tony Nesci said.

"Well, I saved the house, didn't I?" Mom said, laughing.

She sure did, and I was glad. Can you imagine having to start all over again? No, thank you.

With the backyard all burned down, my dad hired an old Italian man who had a horse and a plow. It took a few days for the man to plow the backyard. It was fun to watch. Rocks kept popping up, and my dad saved them so he could use them later to build the wall in front of the house.

After the yard was plowed, the old man attached a contraption made out of chains to the horse where the plow had been. He and the horse pulled the contraption along the ground to make it smooth and flat. Back and forth they went, back and forth. It looked pretty good, until the next day.

Chapter Seven

That night it began to rain—no, not rain, pour. And it was still pouring the next morning. The radio said, "It is a nor'easter," and the streets were full of water.

That morning my mom drove my dad to work and then came home to drive Buddy, Carol Crane, and some of the other neighborhood kids to school. I went with her.

I didn't go to school until the afternoon, so after we dropped everyone off, Mom and I drove up to Fairmount Avenue. The street looked like a huge river. Muddy water was rushing down it.

Mom stopped the car at the corner. She

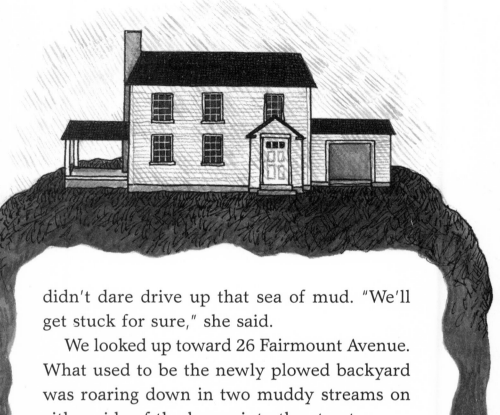

didn't dare drive up that sea of mud. "We'll get stuck for sure," she said.

We looked up toward 26 Fairmount Avenue. What used to be the newly plowed backyard was roaring down in two muddy streams on either side of the house into the street.

"I hope the inside of the house is all right," Mom said.

"We could take our shoes off and go see," I suggested.

"I don't think so," Mom answered. "Your father will just have to check it when he gets home from work."

I was disappointed. I thought it would be fun to squish through all the muddy water.

That night when my dad got home, he told us that everything was fine.

"A little bit of muddy water went into the cellar, but it'll be easy to clean up," Dad said. "But the backyard, well, that's a different story. And the street! The City is going to have to redo the whole street. It's a mess!"

"Oh, no," Mom said. I thought she might start to cry again. But she just said, "I guess that will mean waiting even longer to move into the house."

I sure hoped not. I had just found out about guardian angels from Aunt Nell, my grandfather Tom's sister. Aunt Nell told me that if you wanted something really important, you could ask your guardian angel, and as long as it wasn't a bad thing, you'd probably get it. I figured now was the perfect time to talk to my guardian angel.

And guess what! My guardian angel *did* come to the rescue. The rain stopped. The weather turned cold. Within a week, all that mud on Fairmount Avenue had frozen in place. Cars could go up the street again, and eveyone went back to work on the house.

Finally, the inside stairs were built. I could go upstairs and look at the bedrooms. I could go up to the attic. I could go down to the basement to look at the furnace and see where Mom's laundry room would be. Everything was happening quickly now.

"Looks good," my dad told Buddy and me. "Next time you come here it will be to move in—right after New Year's Eve."

Chapter Eight

Right after New Year's Eve—but first we would have our last Christmas on Columbus Avenue. Dad put up the Santa Claus fireplace for the last time. It was made of cardboard. 26 Fairmount Avenue had a *real* fireplace. Mom put the cotton snow on top of the Santa Claus fireplace and set up the Christmas village.

We had a manger scene, too.

"Next year," Mom said, "we'll get a brand-new manger scene with all new figures for our brand-new house."

On Christmas Eve, the neighbors came by for a party. Mrs. Crane was crying a little. "I'll miss you all next Christmas Eve here on Columbus Avenue." She sniffed. My dad gave her a hug. Carol Crane said she'd miss me, too. Mom said, "Well, you can just all come up the hill to 26 Fairmount Avenue."

It was a great Christmas. Santa brought me an Uncle Wiggly game to go with my Uncle Wiggly books. I got a harmonica and a Jeep doll. The Jeep was an animal from the "Popeye" comics. Buddy got a catcher's mitt and a softball. We got lots of other things, too. Carol Crane got an *authentic* Shirley Temple doll. It was so big and looked so real, I expected it to sing and dance.

On Christmas Day, after church we went to Tom and Nana's house for Christmas dinner. Uncle Charles was there, too, as well as his best friend, Mickey Lynch (we didn't call him Mr.). We had turkey and dressing and gravy.

"Well, Timothy, me bucko (that's what Tom always called me), it won't be long before you're in that nice new house. I'll bet you're excited," Tom said.

Excited? Tom was right.

On New Year's Eve, my mom and dad got all dressed up like movie stars. Mom had on a long black evening gown, with long gloves and silver shoes. Dad wore a tuxedo with a bow tie. They were going to the Wallingford Elks Club New Year's Eve Dance with Uncle Charles and his girlfriend, Viva. Mr. and Mrs. Crane were going to go, too. Carol was going to stay with Buddy and me.

Althea Morin came down from upstairs to take care of us. We were going to have our own New Year's Eve party.

Mom left us brownies and Cokes in the icebox. Mr. and Mrs. Crane gave us party hats and noisemakers to use at midnight.

"Gee," Buddy said, "midnight sure takes a long time coming. I'm going to take a nap—after I drink a Coke and eat some brownies."

Carol, Althea, and I played my new Uncle Wiggly game. We listened to the radio. The doorbell rang, and it was Mr. and Mrs. Morin, Althea's parents, from upstairs. They had a bowl of hot popcorn and some ice cream. "To help celebrate," Mrs. Morin said. Mr. Morin tuned the radio to a program from a fancy nightclub in New York City. "And now," the radio announcer said, "for our entertainment, singing his latest hit, the lilting voice of everyone's favorite Irish tenor, Morton Downey."

Morton Downey was my mom's first cousin. I woke Buddy up.

"Cousin Morton is singing on the radio," I said.

"So what," Buddy said. "Let me sleep."

"You'll miss New Year's," I said.

"I don't care," he said.

"There's ice cream."

"Okay," said Buddy, "I'll get up."

We put on our party hats, drank Cokes, and ate popcorn and ice cream. The radio announcer said, "And now to Times Square. Listen to the crowd, folks. Here we go....Ten, nine, eight, seven, six, five, four, three, two, one—Happy 1940!"

We blew our noisemakers and shouted, "Happy New Year!"

In just a few more days...

Chapter Nine

Everything was crazy. Mom and Dad were packing boxes, packing clothes, running around, saying, "Don't forget the clock" and "Which box does this go in?"

"Here we are, Floss and Joe," some neighbors said, coming in the front door. "Tell us what to do."

"Hi, boys," Uncle Charles called as he drove up in his car. "Ready to go?"

We were going down to Wallingford for the day so we wouldn't be in the way. We were moving—actually moving. I wanted to help; I wanted to see everything. "But think what a big surprise it will be to see your new house all fixed up," Mrs. Crane said to me. Well, maybe she was right.

And I could see that Mom and Dad had a lot to do. Spending the day with Uncle Charles and Mickey Lynch was great. Uncle Charles bought us comic books. We visited Cousin Mabel and her husband, Cousin Bill Powers. We visited Aunt Nell. She made us sandwiches, and tea with sugar and milk for lunch.

"Is it time to go yet?" I asked when we finished eating.

"Not yet," Uncle Charles said.

We went across the street to Tom and Nana's grocery store and spent the afternoon helping them. I put cans of food up on the shelves.

"Now can we go?" I asked. It was beginning to get dark.

"Soon," Uncle Charles told me. "First we're going to have supper."

At Tom and Nana's house we sat in the kitchen, eating at the big kitchen table. It was covered with an oilcloth tablecloth that had pineapples and other fruit on it.

"When can we go?" I asked.

"When your mom calls," Tom said.

Tom read me one of my comic books, and I played with the special wooden blocks that were kept in the sewing room.

Tom, Buddy, Uncle Charles, and I played Chinese Checkers. It was already dark outside.

The telephone rang. I jumped up.

"All right," Nana said. "I'll send them on their way."

Buddy and I ran out to Uncle Charles's car. We picked up his girlfriend, Viva, and Mickey Lynch. And we were on our way.

Through Yalesville, through Tracy, through South Meriden, onto Hanover Street. We turned up Highland Avenue. We drove up the long hill and turned right onto Fairmount Avenue.

The lights were on by the front door of our house. We climbed the makeshift stairs (the real stairs wouldn't be ready until spring).

There on the wall beside the door was a black metal cutout of a tree branch with the silhouette of a squirrel sitting on it. At the end of the branch was the number 26.

56

"Go ahead," Uncle Charles told me. "Push the doorbell." I did.

I heard chimes ring.

The door opened. There was Dad. There was Mom. "Welcome home," they called. "Here's your new house."

I ran in. I ran up the stairs; I ran into my bedroom. There were two brand-new beds, two brand-new dressers, and on the wall a mirror that looked like a ship's wheel. The beds were turned down, and there on the bed nearer the door were my pajamas. It was my bed. It was my room. It was my new house. It was my wonderful home—26 Fairmount Avenue.

The End
(for the time being)

A Note From The Author

Over the years, letters from my young readers have increasingly asked, "When are you going to write a chapter book?" But the idea seemed daunting.

Then one day, my long-time assistant, Bob Hechtel, said, "I have an idea for a chapter book for you—in fact, for a series of chapter books. Why don't you write about all the things that you talk about from your childhood, but can't put into a single picture book." DING—the bell went off—the light bulb lit. "That's it!" I said.

Then the work began. It wasn't hard for me to conjure up all the clear memories I have (and have had for years) of my immediate family and all the friends—and "characters" that surrounded me during my growing up years. Those memories were also re-inforced by hours of home movies that my father and mother took—from little one-year-old Tomie all the way up to movies of me and my dancing partner, Carol Morrissey, with various family/friend outings and siblings along the way.

The real work was to suddenly expand my writing after years of being economical which is essential for my picture books. But I started and with the support of my (also long-time) friend and editor, Margaret Frith, I wrote in an almost stream of consciousness style. Margaret then helped me to organize all the material into this first book. Yes, there will be more. After all, my sisters haven't been born yet, the Second World War hasn't started...enough. Meanwhile, I hope you'll enjoy sharing more of my early life with me, meeting lots of family and other old friends.

Tomie

New Hampshire, 1999